FRESH BEGINNINGS

THE BREAKTHROUGH DEVOTIONAL
for EMOTIONAL HEALING

To: Pastor Jarrett
Bless God for you and your
vision for His people!
Dr. Jones

DR. GWENDOLYN L. PETTWAY, DCC

outskirtspress
DENVER, COLORADO

Contents

Introduction

THE CONCEPT OF Fresh Beginnings was born out of a desire to live an emotionally healthy life. When I gave my life to Christ over thirty years ago, I did not know that living a healthy spiritual life was very dependent on a healthy emotional life. The Apostle Paul tells us in Romans that we are to live a transformed life through the changing of our thoughts. As a Christian counselor, the idea of changing your thoughts to change your behaviors appealed to me. I quickly embraced the concept that my thoughts controlled my emotional health. When I realized that I could heal my emotional pain through changing my mind, I knew I had found the key to emotional healing.

Fresh Beginnings is a daily exercise designed to promote emotional healing. Emotional healing involves a practice of cleansing your mind of past attitudes and thoughts that have kept you from living your very best life. Fresh Beginnings is also a spiritual and mental fast to prepare the mind and soul to enter a new realm of revelation. Fresh Beginnings brings revelation that will release wisdom and fresh insights about your purpose and destiny. God has placed so many gifts inside you. Those gifts are to be used for the building up of His kingdom here on earth. God has also chosen you to participate as a kingdom man or kingdom woman for this hour and for this season.

Soul healing is essential to living a well-balanced life. Soul is made up of three parts: the will, the mind and the emotions. Emotional balance is necessary to help balance the physical body and the spirit. Once our soul realm experiences healing and balance, we are placed in a position to manage our life's concerns. Fresh Beginnings promotes soul healing. Fresh Beginnings promotes self-management. Fresh Beginnings was designed to help you build a devotional life that includes prayer, Bible reading, meditation, and reflection. For the next thirty- one days a topic is introduced, followed by Scripture that supports the topic. Next are words of illumination and a declaration that will inspire you to pray, reflect, and decide what your next best steps are for emotional health. During this season of healing you get to listen to your voice. You also summon the power to erase those negative voices of the past. It is all up to you!

Lastly, a worksheet is included for you to reflect on those areas that need healing. The worksheet is also designed for you to declare the Fresh Beginnings you desire.

Find five to ten minutes each day to go through this daily emotional cleansing. Meditate on the related Scripture. Allow the message of illumination to uplift and encourage you. The message is designed to shine a light of exposure on those painful areas you keep hidden. Repeat the declaration several times during the day as a way of planting new seeds of thought. At the end of your time of daily emotional cleansing, sit silently and wait for God to speak. Press into His presence. You will be amazed at the movement of God and the power of God showing up in your life. Now complete the daily worksheet, making your own declaration for what you want to show up in your life. As a result of this cleansing, you will become a more powerful witness for Christ. You will also become more confident, trusting--and most importantly, more loving. You will be pleasantly surprised at the ease of accepting new perspectives and embracing a fresh beginning daily. You will be blessed. You will be renewed. You will be refreshed! Declare the truth of Fresh Beginnings for your life today…and every day!

#1 Fear Less

"God has not given us the spirit of fear; but of power, and of love, and of a sound mind."
(2 Timothy 1:7)

AS WE PREPARE to move forward in all the blessings God has for us, the first thing to get out of our system is fear. Fear--being afraid--is the number one thought blocker. Fear develops when we try new things, or attempt to step into a different way of thinking and things don't work out as we thought. The more we seemingly "fail," the more we fear that things can't be different. Fear can hold you in its grip for years, and before you know it you've allowed your dreams and hopes to disappear. Sadly, hope seems to be a word just for others. It is fear that comes out of feeling so defeated and in despair.

But there is good news today! Our scripture reminds us that God did not give us that spirit of fear. And God has assured us that when we put our trust in Him, we can live victorious. The mistakes of the past are really stepping stones, or experiences that can help fine-tune our efforts. If we really look at what happened, with the eyes of Christ, we can see that whatever didn't work out made us stronger and wiser. You can test this out for yourself. Look at an experience that you feel didn't work for you. Be honest with yourself--look at what you could have done differently, and now make some new choices. Resolve that you won't make the same choices again. God did not give you that spirit of fear. Today make a choice to give that fear back! Decide that starting today, you will live without fear.

DECLARATION:

Gracious God, I make the decision today to release all fear from my life. You have given me the gifts of confidence and power, and I use those gifts to learn and to teach others. I praise You in advance for this Fresh Beginning.

FRESH BEGINNINGS DAILY WORKSHEET

Really open your heart and allow yourself and God to take a fresh look inside. Allow the light and illumination of the Holy Spirit to shine the light of wholeness and healing into those dark places. It does not matter how long you've been on the journey--there is still a remnant of some hurt or some wound lurking around in the shadows. The following statements will help you ponder today's reading and position you to release any resentment into the hands of Jesus for Him to dispose of as He wishes. Allow yourself enough time to express it all.

I'm angry because:

I regret:

I feel sad when:

I forgive:

Now take time to reflect on today's Scripture. Write out what Jesus is speaking into your spirit:

Today I am grateful for:

My declaration for today:

#2 Faithful

"O love the Lord, all His saints, for the Lord preserves the faithful…."
(Psalms 31:23)

THE FAITHFUL KEEP their hearts open to love for God. Faith full people know that if they always trust in the Lord, He will strengthen them, preserve them, and prosper them. Faithful people don't let thoughts of fear and lack stop them from receiving the blessings of God. Faith full people keep it moving! Faithful people keep it real! Faithful people realize they need God's courage to move ahead. The faithful depend on God's wisdom to make the best choices. The faithful know that trusting in God for strength is the only way to cancel unbelief.

God preserves and keeps our faith full during difficult times. When we or our loved ones are in sickness, it's our faithfulness that helps us to keep standing. And when trouble seems to be the order of the day, we can rest on His promise of grace. Yet no matter what is going on, the faithful know without a shadow of a doubt that God's grace is resting upon them and they will come through as winners! How do we know we win? We win by being plentifully rewarded with love, respect, and courage to walk by faith and not by what we see. We are winners in Christ Who preserves us, no matter what the difficulty or danger. Hallelujah! The things I see may not be what I want them to be, but by faith I know that God will make them what I need them to be. By faith I am encouraged, I am delivered, I am set free. I declare that I am faithful.

DECLARATION:

My God, You are the giver of all that is good. I only need to re-main faithful and proudly do what You instruct me to do. I praise you in advance for preserving me and keeping me while I experience this Fresh Beginning.

FRESH BEGINNINGS DAILY WORKSHEET

Really open your heart and allow yourself and God to take a fresh look inside. Allow the light and illumination of the Holy Spirit to shine the light of wholeness and healing into those dark places. It does not matter how long you've been on the journey--there is still a remnant of some hurt or some wound lurking around in the shadows. The following statements will help you ponder today's reading and position you to release any resentment into the hands of Jesus for Him to dispose of as He wishes. Allow yourself enough time to express it all.

I'm angry because:

I regret:

I feel sad when:

I forgive:

Now take time to reflect on today's Scripture. Write out what Jesus is speaking into your spirit:

Today I am grateful for:

My declaration for today:

#3 From Pressing to Blessing

"Forgetting those things which are behind...I press towards the mark for the prize of the high calling of God in Christ Jesus." (Philippians 3:13-14)

DISCOURAGEMENT, FRUSTRATION, ANGER, unforgiveness, laziness, selfishness, cheapness, contempt, and self-hatred are just a few of the negative attitudes we need to leave behind. God has given us a higher calling. He is calling us to a higher way of thinking, a higher way of doing, a higher way of loving... and even a higher way of cleansing. But before we can actually claim the prize of Fresh Beginnings, we must forget. We must lose consciousness of the things that have kept us bound and living in fear. Today's scripture reminds us that we have to press. In other words, there is a lot of work to do! Pressing begins with taking some serious quality time to examine our thought life to see if it lines up with the thought life of Christ. Christ has high thoughts of hope, love, peace, blessing and grace. Many times we fall short of thinking like Christ because we want to hold someone else responsible for where we have ended up in life. In my past, some things may have been done to me that I couldn't control. Today I realize that I am the only one who can release myself to think higher thoughts of good for myself and for all those around me. In the past I thought someone else was the cause of all my pain and suffering. As an adult, I hold myself accountable for keeping my heart open to all my good.

Starting today, I think on the things of God and His goodness. Today my thoughts are in tune with the blessings and confidence of God. Today I am pressing into my blessing. Today I claim the prize of freedom, joy, and love.

DECLARATION:

Thank You, Lord, for a new and higher way of thinking. Today I press into the blessing of this Fresh Beginning for my life and for those around me. I release the past and embrace the present with high and great expectations for the future.

FRESH BEGINNINGS DAILY WORKSHEET

Really open your heart and allow yourself and God to take a fresh look inside. Allow the light and illumination of the Holy Spirit to shine the light of wholeness and healing into those dark places. It does not matter how long you've been on the journey--there is still a remnant of some hurt or some wound lurking around in the shadows. The following statements will help you ponder today's reading and position you to release any resentment into the hands of Jesus for Him to dispose of as He wishes. Allow yourself enough time to express it all.

I'm angry because:

I regret:

I feel sad when:

I forgive:

Now take time to reflect on today's Scripture. Write out what Jesus is speaking into your spirit:

Today I am grateful for:

My declaration for today:

#4 Forgive

"Who can discern his errors? Forgive my hidden faults." (Psalms 19:12)

WHEN WE THINK of forgiving, usually we think of forgiving someone for an unfair hurt that has been done. Today's exercise involves you forgiving you for the unfair hurt you have done to yourself. Are you wondering how have you been unfair to yourself? Well, think of the times you've lied to yourself. You promised yourself you were going to eat healthier and yet you continued to eat fried foods. Can you believe you betrayed yourself? Think of the many times you have turned your back on yourself. Think again, how you have deceived yourself, cheated yourself, robbed yourself, even been stingy to yourself.

Today, open your eyes and really look at how you have treated yourself. Really look at the hidden stuff you've buried and denied. Today, take a moment and forgive yourself. Take some time--be quiet with yourself, be gentle with yourself, be honest with yourself…but most importantly, love yourself. Love yourself enough to forgive the hurts and mistakes you have made against yourself. Pray for courage to take advantage of this Fresh Beginning today, and make a promise that you will treat yourself fairly, with patience and with honor. Bless yourself today with the gift of forgiveness. Take advantage of the gift of today's new mercy that God offers you. Every day God gives you the opportunity to really examine your intentions…use it to forgive yourself and start without the baggage of yesterday.

DECLARATION:

Bless You, O Lord, for blessing me with the gift of forgiveness. As I forgive others, I forgive myself for how I have transgressed against myself. I graciously receive Your love and care for me, and I forgive myself. Your blessing of Fresh Beginnings is true forgiveness.

FRESH BEGINNINGS DAILY WORKSHEET

Really open your heart and allow yourself and God to take a fresh look inside. Allow the light and illumination of the Holy Spirit to shine the light of wholeness and healing into those dark places. It does not matter how long you've been on the journey--there is still a remnant of some hurt or some wound lurking around in the shadows. The following statements will help you ponder today's reading and position you to release any resentment into the hands of Jesus for Him to dispose of as He wishes. Allow yourself enough time to express it all.

I'm angry because:

I regret:

I feel sad when:

I forgive:

Now return and reflect on today's Scripture. Write out what Jesus is speaking into your spirit:

Today I am grateful for:

My declaration for today:

#5 For Giving

"For God loves a cheerful giver." (2 Corinthians 9:7)

ONE OF THE most important spiritual lessons we must learn is about giving. We learn in John 3:16 that God loved, and then He gave. God gave His best so that we, His disciples, could have. Since Jesus has come, we don't have to "want" for anything. The principle is the same for us today. Giving places us in a position to receive. When we give we are provided for, comforted, and encouraged. When you give financially, it may not always come back in the form of money. That's because God has so many different kinds of blessings in store for us. I am convinced that when we give, that act of selflessness opens our hearts and prepares us to step into the blessings of God, whatever they may be.

Our giving has far-reaching implications. Giving back to God opens up job opportunities, acts of kindness from strangers, miraculous healings, unexpected financial windfalls, peace of mind, unspeakable joy, and so much more. The more we give, the more we receive. The more we give, the more we want to give…for we know God will honor His word to supply our every need. Our God also requires that we give cheerfully. Cheerful giving alerts the Lord that we are trusting in His all-sufficiency with gladness and expectation. We imitate God in giving when we give cheerfully. God gave His son because He knew that we would be reconciled back to Him. God also gave because He knew that the reward of abundant life would be greater than the cost. We cheerfully give to express our thanks and gratitude to God for giving us Jesus.

DECLARATION:

O God, Your act of giving encourages me to give also. I am learning that the more I give, the more I witness Your presence in my life and in the world. Today and every day when I give, I look for ways to give knowing that I will bless and be blessed. Thank You for giving me a Fresh Beginning.

FRESH BEGINNINGS DAILY WORKSHEET

Really open your heart and allow yourself and God to take a fresh look inside. Allow the light and illumination of the Holy Spirit to shine the light of wholeness and healing into those dark places. It does not matter how long you've been on the journey--there is still a remnant of some hurt or some wound lurking around in the shadows. The following statements will help you ponder today's reading and position you to release any resentment into the hands of Jesus for Him to dispose of as He wishes. Allow yourself enough time to express it all.

I'm angry because:

I regret:

I feel sad when:

I forgive:

Now take time to reflect on today's Scripture. Write out what Jesus is speaking into your spirit:

Today I am grateful for:

My declaration for today:

#6 Unbelievable Love

"We know how much God loves us, and we have put our trust in Him." (1 John 3:16)

WE SPEND MUCH of our lives wondering about love: how to love, how to be loved, who loves us, whom do we love? From the very beginning, God demonstrated His love for us in all that He has done for us. But He also shows His love for us in that He cares. Real love says, "I care about the things that affect your life." Caring says, "I will be here to support you." Caring says, "I will defend you, I'll stand up for you, and I'll even carry you." Real love shows us the way, and provides light in darkness, and strength to climb the stairs of challenge. Real love is consistent; it is always there. Real love shows up when we feel our worst and appear to be unlovable. Real love says, "I love you no matter where you've been or what you've done."

So many of us have deep trust issues for a variety of reasons. Somewhere, at some time, we've been let down...even betrayed. However, when we look back over our lives, we see that God has never forsaken us. God's promise is to always be there for us. Now that God's love surrounds us and lives inside of us, we can face this world with confidence. Because of His love, we can demonstrate His love when times are rough. The unbelievable love of God shows up as peace that passes all understanding. For it is His love that keeps, preserves, and sustains our hearts and our minds. There are times when we can't believe the love of God--but today. believe it: it's real.

DECLARATION:

Loving God, Your love is sometimes unbelievable, but I trust in You, for You have never failed me. Your love holds me and lifts me to heights unknown. Your love has loved me into this place of Fresh Beginnings, and I return that love by beginning again.

FRESH BEGINNINGS DAILY WORKSHEET

Really open your heart and allow yourself and God to take a fresh look inside. Allow the light and illumination of the Holy Spirit to shine the light of wholeness and healing into those dark places. It does not matter how long you've been on the journey--there is still a remnant of some hurt or some wound lurking around in the shadows. The following statements will help you ponder today's reading and position you to release any resentment into the hands of Jesus for Him to dispose of as He wishes. Allow yourself enough time to express it all.

I'm angry because:

I regret:

I feel sad when:

I forgive:

Now take time to reflect on today's Scripture. Write out what Jesus is speaking into your spirit:

Today I am grateful for:

My declaration for today:

#7 Grace

"And the God of all grace, who called you to His eternal glory in Christ...." (1 Peter 5:10)

IMAGINE THAT! GOD has called you by His grace into His eternal glory! Are you listening? Can you hear Him calling you, calling your name? When He has settled you and calmed you, you'll hear the call. When you stop the busyness of your agenda, you'll hear the call. God is calling you to live and rest in Him. It's His call that reassures us we can start over and trust in His power and His might. God has called us loved and loveable. He intentionally calls us to help, serve, and minister in His name. In our times of despair He calls for us to come up higher, and enter into His presence. God has called us to shine with the brightness of the eternal glory of Christ. It's by the grace of God that He chose you and called you.

God's grace is free and unconditional. God's grace is unrestricted and always accessible. It is God's grace that abounds and covers. God's grace can always be counted on. God's grace is divine. Grace heals our wounds. Grace delivers and sets free. Grace leads us and follows us. Grace goes before us and makes our way. Grace provides and sustains us. Oh, the grace of God that is mighty and powerful! It is the grace of God that allows us to stand on His promises and to stand in His presence. Grace encourages us to trust in His word and believe. Holy grace! Loving grace! Wonderful grace! Powerful grace! Thank God for His Amazing grace!

DECLARATION:

Gracious God, You've called me to experience the grace of Fresh Beginnings in this earthly walk and grace to bask in the eternal glory in Christ. Thank You for Your gift of grace!

FRESH BEGINNINGS DAILY WORKSHEET

Really open your heart and allow yourself and God to take a fresh look inside. Allow the light and illumination of the Holy Spirit to shine the light of wholeness and healing into those dark places. It does not matter how long you've been on the journey--there is still a remnant of some hurt or some wound lurking around in the shadows. The following statements will help you ponder today's reading and position you to release any resentment into the hands of Jesus for Him to dispose of as He wishes. Allow yourself enough time to express it all.

I'm angry because:

I regret:

I feel sad when:

I forgive:

Now take time to reflect on today's Scripture. Write out what Jesus is speaking into your spirit:

Today I am grateful for:

My declaration for today:

#8 Abundance

"Then Elijah said to Ahab, go up, eat and drink; for there is the sound of abundance of rain."
(1 Kings 18:41)

BEFORE HE ACTUALLY saw the abundance, Elijah heard the sound of abundance first in his spirit. He heard a word of confirmation that what he prayed for was going to happen. What does abundance sound like? How does one hear the sound of abundance? Quite simply, it is through faith. The Bible tells us that faith comes through hearing the word of God. And we have all heard at some time in our spiritual journey that God will supply our every need. So it is our faith that hears abundance. It is our faith to believe the impossible. We need faith to trust in God's wisdom. It takes faith to leave a bad situation with nothing and end up with everything you need. It takes faith to return to school in your forties and sail on through to a PhD. It takes faith to start a business with a few dollars and be able to pay for your children's college education.

You get it now? I heard this somewhere: "God doesn't respond to your needs; He responds to your faith." God already knows what we need. He is waiting on your faith and my faith to call those needs into existence. Elijah needed rain, but it was his faith in an unfailing God that caused an abundance to come forth. Well, while waiting on the manifestation, Elijah surely knew the rain was coming, because he gave his servant instructions. Get prepared for the abundance. Start celebrating in advance for the abundance. If God said it, it's going to happen. Go ahead--eat and drink, because the rain symbolizes cleansing and a refreshing. The rain symbolizes Fresh Beginnings! Look for the outpourings of abundance!

DECLARATION:

Heavenly Father, thank You for the faith to hear the sound of my abundance. As I think on Your goodness and the provision of Your storehouse, I can rest assured that You will not withhold any good thing from me. Today I hear the sound of abundance, and it is the sound of Fresh Beginnings.

FRESH BEGINNINGS DAILY WORKSHEET

Really open your heart and allow yourself and God to take a fresh look inside. Allow the light and illumination of the Holy Spirit to shine the light of wholeness and healing into those dark places. It does not matter how long you've been on the journey--there is still a remnant of some hurt or some wound lurking around in the shadows. The following statements will help you ponder today's reading and position you to release any resentment into the hands of Jesus for Him to dispose of as He wishes. Allow yourself enough time to express it all.

I'm angry because:

I regret:

I feel sad when:

I forgive:

Now take time to reflect on today's Scripture. Write out what Jesus is speaking into your spirit:

Today I am grateful for:

My declaration for today:

#9 Healed

"By His stripes we are healed." (Isaiah 53:5)

WOULD YOU BELIEVE that for every illness there is a stripe that covers it? There is healing in every stripe that Jesus took for us. He was wounded that we would be healed. He took forty stripes so that nothing would be left uncovered. There is a stripe for cancer, bronchitis, lupus, and drug addiction. Whatever your concerns are, Jesus received a stripe for it.

It is through our faith that we access the healing stripe for whatever illness attacks us. It took the power and presence of God for Jesus to claim healing for us. It will take the power and presence of God to receive our healing. We too must have our minds focused on the healing we desire. Oh, yes--it will take some effort on our part. We must constantly cry out, pray, meditate, walk in obedience, exercise, eat healthy...and most importantly, forgive. What Jesus requires of us is nothing compared to the pain He endured for us. Jesus boldly took each and every stripe. He let His accusers lash Him across His back until His flesh was torn to pieces. While His back was being torn apart, His mind was focused on how we could be whole. His life was jeopardized so that we could live in health. He agreed to pay the price of suffering so that we would not suffer. It was the ultimate act of selflessness. He knew that for every agonizing crack of the whip that landed on Him, some child would breathe easier. Jesus bore a stripe so that one blood cell would not overtake another. Jesus took a stripe so that a sad soul could finally sleep through the night. With every snap of the whip, Jesus took a stripe so that we could be healed in our bodies, healed in our minds--and yes, healed in our souls. Picture this...in every snap of the whip, Jesus bent over so that we could stand up straight.

DECLARATION:

Jesus, I'll never forget what You've done for me. When I want to complain, I only need to see You bent over taking those lashes so that I could be healed. There is a Fresh Beginning in every bloody stripe. Today I receive my healing.

FRESH BEGINNINGS DAILY WORKSHEET

Really open your heart and allow yourself and God to take a fresh look inside. Allow the light and illumination of the Holy Spirit to shine the light of wholeness and healing into those dark places. It does not matter how long you've been on the journey there is still a remnant of some hurt or some wound lurking around in the shadows. The following statements will help you ponder today's reading and position you to release any resentment into the hands of Jesus for Him to dispose of as He wishes. Allow yourself enough time to express it all.

I'm angry because:

I regret:

I feel sad when:

I forgive:

Now take time to reflect on today's Scripture. Write out what Jesus is speaking into your spirit:

Today I am grateful for:

My declaration for today:

#10 Joy

"Who for the joy set before him…." (Hebrews 12:2)

JESUS ENDURED AND was despised, only to finally grab hold of the joy to come--the joy of knowing that after death there is life. Jesus experienced a literal death, and the joy for Him was to be reunited in Glory with God. But His joy was also for us to know that we too would now have an advocate to make sure we would enter that same Glory. There's another place in the Bible that reminds us that sorrow may endure for a night but joy comes in the morning. What we're seeing here is that we must go through some difficult days before we can delight in the joy. Without challenges and difficulties, we could not experience the depth of joy. Without some dark moments, we would not even recognize the moments of light.

   Happiness may begin and end with a specific event. Joy is more than happiness, in that it lasts longer, it is more permanent. Joy is present whether we feel it or not. It's amazing that we can have joy and be joyful while going through our challenges. The Bible reminds us that God promised us the peace that passes all understanding. You may not understand why you are without a job, going through a divorce, feeling isolated from friends…and yet God promised that whatever we go through, there is joy set before us.

   Joy is the goal--it's the main objective; it is the end result of suffering. While we can be happy and relieved that a painful event is over, joy says, "Even while I go through the painful event, I am joyful. I am joyful because I trust in the promise that God will always be with me." God has set joy before us. We only have to reach for it through faith.

DECLARATION:

Thank You, Lord, for joy that is reachable and obtainable. I continue to reach for the joy of trusting in Your faithfulness. I continue to trust in the promise that trouble won't last always. Thank You, Father, that even as I go through, there is a Fresh Beginning set before me.

FRESH BEGINNINGS DAILY WORKSHEET

Really open your heart and allow yourself and God to take a fresh look inside. Allow the light and illumination of the Holy Spirit to shine the light of wholeness and healing into those dark places. It does not matter how long you've been on the journey--there is still a remnant of some hurt or some wound lurking around in the shadows. The following statements will help you ponder today's reading and position you to release any resentment into the hands of Jesus for Him to dispose of as He wishes. Allow yourself enough time to express it all.

I'm angry because:

I regret:

I feel sad when:

I forgive:

Now take time to reflect on today's Scripture. Write out what Jesus is speaking into your spirit:

Today I am grateful for:

My declaration for today:

#11 Only a Look

"But when he saw the wind, he was afraid…." (Matthew 14:30)

CAN YOU REMEMBER the first time you saw the evidence of Jesus' presence in your life? For many, there was the sense of being renewed, restored--and yes, born again. You may have even felt hopeful that a fresh beginning was taking place. Oh, how we welcomed that new wind and the joy of knowing that we wouldn't have to carry our burdens alone! Only a look at Jesus and what He promises brings so much peace. Only a look at Jesus gives courage and strength. Only a look at Jesus brings healing to a weary soul. Only a look at Jesus inspires us to take it to the next level. Only a look at Jesus calms our fears. Only a look at Jesus brings relief.

For a moment, Peter stopped looking at Jesus, and he began to sink. But Jesus never stopped looking at Peter. He never took His eyes off of Peter. It was only a look from Jesus that saved Peter from drowning. Only a look from Jesus keeps us above water. Only a look from Jesus sees us through the dark nights of our souls. Only a look from Jesus keeps us grounded in faith to believe. Only a look from Jesus forgives. Only a look from Jesus sets us free. Only a look at the blood of Jesus reminds God that we are covered. Only a look at the resurrection reminds us of our Mediator who continues to advocate for us. Only a look at the living Word and you remember there is no reason to fear. We may take our eyes off Jesus, but He never takes His eyes off of us.

◀ **FRESH BEGINNINGS**

DECLARATION:

Bless You, Lord, for always keeping watch over my life. I rejoice that only a look from You keeps me from drowning in the sea of life's troubled waters. I praise You for a look of love that assures me of Your power and presence in my life. It is the look of Fresh Beginnings.

FRESH BEGINNINGS DAILY WORKSHEET

Really open your heart and allow yourself and God to take a fresh look inside. Allow the light and illumination of the Holy Spirit to shine the light of wholeness and healing into those dark places. It does not matter how long you've been on the journey--there is still a remnant of some hurt or some wound lurking around in the shadows. The following statements will help you ponder today's reading and position you to release any resentment into the hands of Jesus for Him to dispose of as He wishes. Allow yourself enough time to express it all.

I'm angry because:

I regret:

I feel sad when:

I forgive:

Now take time to reflect on today's Scripture. Write out what Jesus is speaking into your spirit:

Today I am grateful for:

My declaration for today:

#12 It's in the Cup

"But Jesus answered...are you able to drink from the bitter cup...?" (Mark 10:38)

CAN YOU DRINK from the cup? Have you counted the cost of what's in the cup? Are you willing to lay down your life, your hopes, your dreams, your ambitions for the glory of God? Some of you are saying yes without even looking to see what's in the cup. Jesus had the good sense to know it wasn't about Him and His desires to be great, but it was about God's desire to use His life for greatness--and believe it or not greatness, is in the cup. Greatness, for the believer, would be the sharing of Christ's lot with Him, an agreement of suffering between the believer and Christ. Drinking of the cup of the Lord involves much more than just partaking of a cup of wine at a communion table.

When we are chosen to serve, it also shows our solidarity with Christ in His ministry. When Christ asked His disciples if they could drink from the cup, He was asking them if they had the faith to really follow Him. Would they be willing to pay the price of true discipleship? He was telling them that there is no crown without a cross.

Jesus reminds us that in this world you will have your hard times--there will be some difficult days ahead. Sometimes you will cry and want to quit. The good news is to be encouraged, for Christ has overcome the world. The great news is that although trying times are in the cup, Fresh Beginnings are also in the cup. For after you have suffered, you shall also reign. Do not fear; look in the cup. See what's in it for you.

DECLARATION:

Dear God, up until now I've been afraid to look in the cup. But today I realize that Your promise of strength and power is also in the cup. I drink from the cup willingly and freely. I owe You the glory for the cup of Fresh Beginnings.

FRESH BEGINNINGS DAILY WORKSHEET

Really open your heart and allow yourself and God to take a fresh look inside. Allow the light and illumination of the Holy Spirit to shine the light of wholeness and healing into those dark places. It does not matter how long you've been on the journey--there is still a remnant of some hurt or some wound lurking around in the shadows. The following statements will help you ponder today's reading and position you to release any resentment into the hands of Jesus for Him to dispose of as He wishes. Allow yourself enough time to express it all.

I'm angry because:

I regret:

I feel sad when:

I forgive:

Now take time to reflect on today's Scripture. Write out what Jesus is speaking into your spirit:

Today I am grateful for:

My declaration for today:

#13 My Worship is for Real

"God is spirit, and His worshipers must worship in spirit and truth."
(John 4:24)

HOW DOES ONE become a worshipper? One must first know that worship is for God only--not only for what He has done, but for who He is. In worship God reveals who He is. In worship God also reveals the intimate details and plans for our lives. God must be held in the highest adoration as the sustainer of all life. Without God, there is no me or you. With God, we live and move and breathe. When we worship God, we assume an attitude of faith, and in prayer we begin to press into His presence.

Worship is work, as we intentionally move out of and beyond the cares of this world and seek the presence of God. In real worship, we no longer seek the approval of man. In real worship we seek the power of God to live a transformed life. In real worship we desire fresh beginnings, fresh favor, and fresh anointing. In real worship we seek only to connect deeply and totally with God. In real worship we strive to listen, wait, and long only for God. Jesus told the Samaritan woman: "A time is coming...when true worshipers will worship the Father in spirit and in truth, for they are the kind of worshipers the Father seeks." Isn't that remarkable? As we seek God's presence, He is also seeking our presence. Now, when we connect with God, mighty and powerful things begin to happen. Our faces shine brightly, showing the world that we sought and found the face of God. We'll look at our hands, and they will look new; we'll look at our feet, and they'll look new too. Our talk and our walk will be changed…all for God's glory. It is when our worship is for real that we come into knowledge of the truth.

DECLARATION:

God, I adore You and honor You in worship. Please accept my worship and allow me to enter into Your presence, for only in Your presence I can be made whole. In Your presence is a Fresh Beginning that only You can give.

FRESH BEGINNINGS DAILY WORKSHEET

Really open your heart and allow yourself and God to take a fresh look inside. Allow the light and illumination of the Holy Spirit to shine the light of wholeness and healing into those dark places. It does not matter how long you've been on the journey--there is still a remnant of some hurt or some wound lurking around in the shadows. The following statements will help you ponder today's reading and position you to release any resentment into the hands of Jesus for Him to dispose of as He wishes. Allow yourself enough time to express it all.

I'm angry because:

I regret:

I feel sad when:

I forgive:

Now take time to reflect on today's Scripture. Write out what Jesus is speaking into your spirit:

Today I am grateful for:

My declaration for today:

#14 Divine Connection

"The Lord our God made a covenant with us...." (Deuteronomy 5:2)

MANY TIMES WE place a lot of emphasis on who we know. We look to people who we feel will do the most for us. We seek out those who will provide us with some special connection. We love to drop names to impress others and make ourselves look grand. We desire to connect to those of a perceived higher status in the world so that we too can claim: "I am somebody." Those kinds of connections can be dangerous as we try to hook up with someone, anyone who will pay us some attention. The danger in this is that we become desperate. Our vision and judgment become cloudy, and before we know it we're hooked up with the wrong people. We wear the newest or most expensive designer labels. Some even rent designer handbags and luggage to show how connected they are. Sadly, we often get involved with people who have hidden agendas...only to have our own hidden agendas exposed.

Judas hooked up with Jesus for all the wrong reasons. Judas got caught up in his own game by trying to connect with Jesus and stay connected with his old gang. The Bible warns of straddling the fence, also known as being lukewarm. Judas sold his life for a worthless connection. Let me remind you today: there is only one true connection, and it is a divine connection. This connection won't disappoint or let you down. It will always be genuine; it will always be the real thing! Jesus gives us the one solid connection to God. God is in covenant with us. He has promised to stay connected to us. With this divine connection, I don't have to dress in designer labels to look important. I don't have to drop any worldly names. I only have to call on the name of Jesus--and just like that, I'm connected!

DECLARATION:

Mighty God, I am strengthened today by my divine connection to You. I am experiencing Fresh Beginnings only because of Jesus, Who is the connecting source to Your power and Your might. I receive the blessing of divine connection.

FRESH BEGINNINGS DAILY WORKSHEET

Really open your heart and allow yourself and God to take a fresh look inside. Allow the light and illumination of the Holy Spirit to shine the light of wholeness and healing into those dark places. It does not matter how long you've been on the journey--there is still a remnant of some hurt or some wound lurking around in the shadows. The following statements will help you ponder today's reading and position you to release any resentment into the hands of Jesus for Him to dispose of as He wishes. Allow yourself enough time to express it all.

I'm angry because:

I regret:

I feel sad when:

I forgive:

Now take time to reflect on today's Scripture. Write out what Jesus is speaking into your spirit:

Today I am grateful for:

My declaration for today:

#15 The Blessing

"For I know the plans I have for you,' declares the Lord. Plans to prosper you...plans to give you hope and a future." (Jeremiah 29:11)

WHEN SOMEONE MAKES a declaration, it is a statement made full of intention and promise. A declaration is made when you are sure beyond a shadow of a doubt that what you say will happen; it WILL come to pass.

Many of us are afraid to declare a thing for fear that our words will return void. We lack the confidence needed to speak or declare a thing, knowing it will be established. Let us take our cue from God Himself, Who declares that He knows the plans He has for you and me. In other words, He is clear and very clear about His intentions. He makes it clear to us when He declares that we will prosper. If you're not feeling or receiving this declaration, go back and read it again and again until you get it. You need to get that in your spirit right now...you are destined for prosperity! God takes it a step further and declares His plans to give you hope. If God says He's giving you hope...then believe it! Act on it! Even when it looks like all hope is gone, go back and read it again. God is giving hope! Now this is the real kicker. Our past may be filled with lack, poverty, hopelessness, and any other negative thing the enemy threw at us. But that was then and this is now. God has plans for your future. It is a future that is filled with the brightness of His love and power. Your future is full of favor. God has declared the blessing on your life. It is the blessing of Fresh Beginnings.

DECLARATION:

Hallelujah! I receive the blessing today. Thank You, God, for looking ahead and declaring plans of prosperity, hope, and a future for me. Thank You, Lord, for declaring the Blessing of Fresh Beginnings!

FRESH BEGINNINGS DAILY WORKSHEET

Really open your heart and allow yourself and God to take a fresh look inside. Allow the light and illumination of the Holy Spirit to shine the light of wholeness and healing into those dark places. It does not matter how long you've been on the journey--there is still a remnant of some hurt or some wound lurking around in the shadows. The following statements will help you ponder today's reading and position you to release any resentment into the hands of Jesus for Him to dispose of as He wishes. Allow yourself enough time to express it all.

I'm angry because:

I regret:

I feel sad when:

I forgive:

Now take time to reflect on today's Scripture. Write out what Jesus is speaking into your spirit:

Today I am grateful for:

My declaration for today:

#16 Holiness

"The Lord will show who belongs to Him and who is holy, and He will have that person come near Him." (Numbers 16:5)

YOU KNOW. I know. Jesus knows. We know that in our natural state we are not worthy to stand in the presence of a Holy God. Yet the invitation is always there to "Come unto me...." We have a standing invitation to always present ourselves before God and commune with Him. At first thought it seems strange that a Holy God would want us to be in His presence. Yet we've experienced the awesome, wonderful, and magnificent presence of God many times and in many ways in our lives.

The holiness of God can seem frightening. The guilt and shame we feel makes us afraid to come to Him. We wonder how we, with our shortcomings, can even have a thought to talk to God. Yet He has offered us a way, through Jesus, to come confidently into His presence. The righteousness of Jesus is the righteousness that God sees in us. That righteousness opens up the way to enter into His space. It's the righteousness of Jesus that gives us the right to stare in His face. God knew there was nothing we could do to cleanse ourselves, make ourselves right, make ourselves better, or get it together so that God could accept us. God knows our hearts are not always full of love. God knows it is difficult for us to live holy all the time. Some days we feel we're doing everything just right. Then there are days we know we blow it. So Jesus agreed to stand in the gap for us and fulfill the requirements of reconciliation. At the moment that Jesus died, that holy contract was stamped--it is finished! That finished work assures our Fresh Beginnings.

DECLARATION:

Holy God, thank You that your holiness is not a threat, but a welcome place of refuge. It is a place where I can sit at Your feet and contemplate the Fresh Beginnings of holiness.

FRESH BEGINNINGS DAILY WORKSHEET

Really open your heart and allow yourself and God to take a fresh look inside. Allow the light and illumination of the Holy Spirit to shine the light of wholeness and healing into those dark places. It does not matter how long you've been on the journey--there is still a remnant of some hurt or some wound lurking around in the shadows. The following statements will help you ponder today's reading and position you to release any resentment into the hands of Jesus for Him to dispose of as He wishes. Allow yourself enough time to express it all.

I'm angry because:

I regret:

I feel sad when:

I forgive:

Now take time to reflect on today's Scripture. Write out what Jesus is speaking into your spirit:

Today I am grateful for:

My declaration for today:

#17 Prayer and Power

"And pray in the Spirit on all occasions with all kinds of prayers and requests." (Ephesians 6:18a)

WE HAVE THIS saying at our church: "No prayer, no power; little prayer, little power; much prayer, much power!" Over the years we have come to know the power in prayer. We are persuaded that to witness the movement of God in our lives, we must have a powerful and consistent prayer life. Prayer requires that we fall on our face as we seek the face of God. Prayer requires that we press into God's presence. An extremely important aspect of prayer is that we empty ourselves of the stuff that separates us from God. We press, we wait, and we empty ourselves until all outer distractions become silent and we become attuned to the voice of God. The purpose of prayer is to hear the voice of God. We want to hear what God is speaking to us, how God is directing us, and what God wants to do in our lives. It is that powerful word from God that will cause the necessary shifting and realignments to move us into the next level of our purpose and destiny.

Let us press into God's presence, and let us stay there until we get the answers that we need. There will not be a healing or a shifting until we pray. There will not be a movement until we cultivate a prayer life. Our prayer life gives us power, much power, to cause heaven to shake and release the blessings of God. Not just power for houses, or cars, or more money…but power to witness God's glory.

We need power to pray so that men and women turn to Jesus as their Lord. We need prayer power that releases revelatory understanding of God's activity. We must pray to come into agreement with God and His agenda. We must pray to shut down every spirit of division and discord. Listen--we must pray for power to take care of God's business, knowing He will take care of ours. Remember...much prayer, much power!

DECLARATION:

God, we seek Your face through prayer, and we stay on our face until we hear from you. Speak a word that will encourage and enlighten us to receive Your blessing. Let us pray for the blessing of Fresh Beginnings.

FRESH BEGINNINGS DAILY WORKSHEET

Really open your heart and allow yourself and God to take a fresh look inside. Allow the light and illumination of the Holy Spirit to shine the light of wholeness and healing into those dark places. It does not matter how long you've been on the journey--there is still a remnant of some hurt or some wound lurking around in the shadows. The following statements will help you ponder today's reading and position you to release any resentment into the hands of Jesus for Him to dispose of as He wishes. Allow yourself enough time to express it all.

I'm angry because:

I regret:

I feel sad when:

I forgive:

Now take time to and reflect on today's Scripture. Write out what Jesus is speaking into your spirit:

Today I am grateful for:

My declaration for today:

#18 180°

"Repent then, turn to God, so that your sins may be wiped out, that times of refreshing may come from the Lord." (Acts 3:19)

LET'S TALK ABOUT repentance. Why repent? Repentance releases the anointing. We need the anointing to:
     Destroy every yoke
     Break every chain of bondage
     Bind up every spirit of judgment and condemnation
     Release us from every lie the enemy has told us
     Release us from living the lie of someone else's journey

Peter encourages us to repent so that our sins may be wiped out. Repentance is needed to release times of refreshing and Fresh Beginnings. True repentance is not just turning around. If you are facing your sin, challenge, or obstacle turning around, making a 360° turn, just brings you face to face with it again. But when you make a 180° degree turn, you are no longer presented with the challenge of embracing that sin again. You turn your back to that sin. A 180° degree turn also signifies that you have changed your mind. So repentance is really changing your mind. Turning 180° is turning away from the thing that is keeping you in tension with God's will. Turning 180° says you turn your back on the thing that keeps you out of step. Only you have the power to change your mind. You can declare today that you will think differently about yourself, the people in your life, your relationship to others--and most importantly, your relationship to God.

Repent--make that 180° degree turn, and turn to God. God has your back, so don't worry about what's behind you. Turn to God for the refreshing. Turn to God for Fresh Beginnings.

DECLARATION:

Today I turn my back on negative attitudes, old habits, low self-esteem, and being unmanageable. I repent by turning away from the past. I turn to God and receive the anointing to embrace the power of a 180° turn to Fresh Beginnings.

FRESH BEGINNINGS DAILY WORKSHEET

Really open your heart and allow yourself and God to take a fresh look inside. Allow the light and illumination of the Holy Spirit to shine the light of wholeness and healing into those dark places. It does not matter how long you've been on the journey--there is still a remnant of some hurt or some wound lurking around in the shadows. The following statements will help you ponder today's reading and position you to release any resentment into the hands of Jesus for Him to dispose of as He wishes. Allow yourself enough time to express it all.

I'm angry because:

I regret:

I feel sad when:

I forgive:

Now take time to reflect on today's Scripture. Write out what Jesus is speaking into your spirit:

Today I am grateful for:

My declaration for today:

#19 Rahab…On Assignment

"Agreed, she replied, let it be as you say…and she tied the scarlet cord in the window."
(Joshua 2:21)

WHEN YOU FIRST hear the name of Rahab many of you also think "prostitute." Yes, that is how the Bible identifies her for this story. Go back and read her story again. Rahab went from being a prostitute to being a special agent in a moment. God entrusted an assignment to her. Do you think God forgot she was a prostitute? When the spies came to her home she was a "working girl." She was right in the middle of her mess. He didn't wait until she got herself together. God took Rahab's mess and turned it into a message. Rahab used her gift of "negotiation" and was able to secure a plan of salvation for her family. She was not afraid to sit at the table and map out a plan that would place her name in God's hall of fame. She was a visionary, for she saw that if she cooperated, she could see blessings down the road for her and her family. When the spies told her who they were and what they wanted, she accepted the assignment and became a special agent for God. You can believe that she guarded that assignment fiercely. She knew what was at stake. Most importantly, she heard what God had done--and she believed. She became a believer and God honored her belief. The end of the story says she married a prince and went from prostitute to princess. Only God. Only God can place you on special assignment and change your life forever.

DECLARATION:

Today I declare that I am on special assignment for the Lord. I use the gifts He has given me to help others. My gifts open the door of Fresh Beginnings.

FRESH BEGINNINGS DAILY WORKSHEET

Really open your heart and allow yourself and God to take a fresh look inside. Allow the light and illumination of the Holy Spirit to shine the light of wholeness and healing into those dark places. It does not matter how long you've been on the journey--there is still a remnant of some hurt or some wound lurking around in the shadows. The following statements will help you ponder today's reading and position you to release any resentment into the hands of Jesus for Him to dispose of as He wishes. Allow yourself enough time to express it all.

I'm angry because:

I regret:

I feel sad when:

I forgive:

Now take time to reflect on today's Scripture. Write out what Jesus is speaking into your spirit:

Today I am grateful for:

My declaration for today:

#20 Nevertheless

"My Father…yet not as I will, but as You will." (Matthew 26:39)

PICTURE THIS: JESUS is in the Garden of Gethsemane, praying… praying so hard, until His sweat resembles drops of blood. He was facing the biggest challenge in His life. Should He save His life, or die to save the world? Although many of us may not be faced with the decision to give up our physical life for some greater good, we are asked to die spiritually every day. Dying spiritually is for our greater good and for the good of others. To die spiritually is to surrender. We surrender our cause to be popular, the most beautiful, the smartest, or whatever need you are trying to fulfill with worldly supports.

When Jesus said nevertheless, He meant "Not My will, not My cause, not My perspective, not My goal, not My plan, not My way." He also meant that His will was never anything less than what God wanted.

Are you faced with a situation that if you simply surrendered and declared "nevertheless," God can have His way in your life? When you allow God's way over your way, you align yourself with His plan. Surrender your desire to always be right. Surrender your selfishness. Surrender your arrogance. Declare "nevertheless," so that you kill that thing that is standing in the way of a deeper connection with God. Declaring "nevertheless" opens the way for fresh beginnings.

DECLARATION: Father I give up my "never" for Your "nevertheless" to usher in the work of a Fresh Beginning in my life.

FRESH BEGINNINGS DAILY WORKSHEET

Really open your heart and allow yourself and God to take a fresh look inside. Allow the light and illumination of the Holy Spirit to shine the light of wholeness and healing into those dark places. It does not matter how long you've been on the journey--there is still a remnant of some hurt or some wound lurking around in the shadows. The following statements will help you ponder today's reading and position you to release any resentment into the hands of Jesus for Him to dispose of as He wishes. Allow yourself enough time to express it all.

I'm angry because:

I regret:

I feel sad when:

I forgive:

Now take time to and reflect on today's Scripture. Write out what Jesus is speaking into your spirit:

Today I am grateful for:

My declaration for today:

#21 Trust God First

"Fear of man will prove to be a snare, but whoever trusts in the Lord will be kept safe."
(Proverbs 29:25)

I'VE LEARNED TO trust God first in everything. People come and go, they don't show up, promises are not kept, people disappoint. But when I put my trust in God first, the disappointments, the unkept promises, the coming and going are that much easier to handle.

Trusting God first is the sure way to keep the door of Fresh Beginnings open and accessible. When I trust God first, I decrease the time spent worrying about the what-ifs, and the shoulda, coulda, woulda. Trusting God first gives me the security and the assurance of a rock-solid foundation in Christ. When I trust God first, I am less critical of myself and less judgmental of others. When I trust God first, I am amazed at my level of patience with others and especially myself. When I trust God first, I can wait on God, knowing that in times of stress my strength will be renewed.

Putting my trust in God first also reminds me to "see others (and myself) through the eyes of Christ" and then I'm reminded that we are all doing the best we can. Trusting God first encourages me to remember that God is the head of my life. Trusting God first helps me to remember not to set my expectations so high for myself and others that we cannot reach them. When I trust God first, I may feel lonely, but I know the truth that I'm never alone. When in doubt, I know I can look to the hills where my help come from. Trusting God first decreases my frustrations when I want to run ahead of God and do things my way. When I trust God first I take authority over anxiety that causes me to become unmanageable. Take the pressure off of yourself and others--and trust God first!

DECLARATION:

Dear God, I know I cannot experience Fresh Beginnings without trusting You first. I put my trust in You first as I release all fear.

FRESH BEGINNINGS DAILY WORKSHEET

Really open your heart and allow yourself and God to take a fresh look inside. Allow the light and illumination of the Holy Spirit to shine the light of wholeness and healing into those dark places. It does not matter how long you've been on the journey--there is still a remnant of some hurt or some wound lurking around in the shadows. The following statements will help you ponder today's reading and position you to release any resentment into the hands of Jesus for Him to dispose of as He wishes. Allow yourself enough time to express it all.

I'm angry because:

I regret:

I feel sad when:

I forgive:

Now take time to and reflect on today's Scripture. Write out what Jesus is speaking into your spirit:

Today I am grateful for:

My declaration for today:

#22 It's Time

"But I pray to You O, Lord, in the time of Your favor…answer me with Your sure salvation." (Psalms 69:13)

WHILE DRIVING, WE look forward through the front windshield to maneuver through traffic to reach our destination. We occasionally glance in the rearview mirror to make sure things behind us are clear--for example, that we are not in the path of an ambulance or police chase. Imagine the disaster if we constantly looked in the rearview mirror while navigating through traffic.

The same could be said of the way we look at our life. We can choose to look forward with hope and trust in the strategic road map God has designed for us. It's time to decide to look forward. We spend far too much time looking back at the hurts, the mistakes of the past, and memories of the "good old days," and we miss the brightness of the future that lies in front of us.

It's time to break free of the chains that keep us tied to a past that has no power to set us free. The only purpose the past serves is a reminder that we're still here, that we have new opportunities to try again. It's time to take God seriously. It's time to make room and space for God. This is a time of God's favor. It's time to trust the sure salvation of God. It's time to let God's rule, reign, and influence become the compass that directs us to the next level of Fresh Beginnings.

DECLARATION:

Father, it's time I release myself from dwelling in a past that keeps me tied up, tangled and bound up. I intentionally look forward to the Fresh Beginnings of a future filled with the favor You have planned for me.

FRESH BEGINNINGS DAILY WORKSHEET

Really open your heart and allow yourself and God to take a fresh look inside. Allow the light and illumination of the Holy Spirit to shine the light of wholeness and healing into those dark places. It does not matter how long you've been on the journey--there is still a remnant of some hurt or some wound lurking around in the shadows. The following statements will help you ponder today's reading and position you to release any resentment into the hands of Jesus for Him to dispose of as He wishes. Allow yourself enough time to express it all.

I'm angry because:

I regret:

I feel sad when:

I forgive:

Now take time to reflect on today's Scripture. Write out what Jesus is speaking into your spirit:

Today I am grateful for:

My declaration for today:

#23 In My Mind

"Let this mind be in you, which was also in Christ Jesus." (Philippians 2:5)

HAVE YOU EVER noticed that when you are talking to people and they are trying to make a point of influence they will most often say, "Well, in my mind…" or "This is my thing"? One of the things people fail to realize is that they are doing exactly that: they are speaking from their mind's point of view. The point they are making is based on their own perspective. It's amusing that if it is in their mind, and it is true for them, then it must be true for everyone. I once talked to a person who exclaimed, "Why can't they all just think like me?" Many feel that their way of thinking is the only way to think about things.

A wife is talking about a concern with her husband and she says, "In my mind, he is being rude and insensitive." The husband looks at her in disbelief because that is the farthest thing from his mind. As long as you stay in your mind, you cannot tap into the mind of God. When we learn to have the mind of Christ, we can learn to still our minds so that we become mindful of what the other is really saying to us. David asks the question of God: "Who is man that you are mindful of him?" What David realized--and hopefully we will too--is that when God's mind is mindful of us, we should take note that His thoughts toward us are always full of goodness and compassion. We never have to guess, wonder, or make up our own perspectives. God is clear, and He can be trusted.

It is a privilege when others take the time to share their thoughts with us. We can learn to become still and mindful. We can remember to breathe, listen, and pay attention even when the discussion is difficult. Now you may say to God, "This is how I see things; he was wrong, she treated me badly, or I'm such a mess."

God says, "But in My mind, you are beautiful, forgiven, loved, and chosen."

DECLARATION:

Dear God, in my mind I plant the seeds of mindfulness. I receive Your thoughts of Fresh Beginnings.

FRESH BEGINNINGS DAILY WORKSHEET

Really open your heart and allow yourself and God to take a fresh look inside. Allow the light and illumination of the Holy Spirit to shine the light of wholeness and healing into those dark places. It does not matter how long you've been on the journey--there is still a remnant of some hurt or some wound lurking around in the shadows. The following statements will help you ponder today's reading and position you to release any resentment into the hands of Jesus for Him to dispose of as He wishes. Allow yourself enough time to express it all.

I'm angry because:

I regret:

I feel sad when:

I forgive:

Now take time to reflect on today's Scripture. Write out what Jesus is speaking into your spirit:

Today I am grateful for:

My declaration for today:

#24 Positioned for Purpose

"You will not have to fight this battle. Take up your positions; stand firm and see the deliverance the Lord will give you. (2 Chronicles 20:17)

POSITION – TO put or arrange (someone or something) in a particular place or way.

Purpose – the reason for which something is done or created or for which something exists.

When we put those two definitions together spiritually, we find that God has put or arranged us in a particular place for His intention, His plan, His design...His purpose. God is saying to us that He has an intentional plan for our lives and all that we go through, the good and the difficult, is shaping us for our purpose. Many of us are yet crying out, "Lord what is my purpose? Where should I be and what should I do?"

I want to add that position is more than a physical stance. It is also mental, always spiritual and most definitely emotional. When you continue to look at the dynamics of your life from a negative attitude, your position is one of defeat. When you wonder where is God in the chaos of your life, spiritually your position is weakened because of unbelief. Now your position is compromised because you are off track and out of control. The way you think about your situation and how you think about God are affecting your purpose. If you continue to think negatively and in defeat, you are out of God's positioning for your purpose. When you can change your mind to think like an adult--not just someone who is of age chronologically, but with maturity--you get back in position to realize your purpose. Walking in your purpose involves a mature mindset: a mindset that is honest, genuine, and complete with integrity. A mature mindset is governed by responsibility and accountability. Leaving childish things behind is one of the major changes we can make to stay in position. Putting away childish attitudes of tantrums, pouting, selfishness, and wanting things our way are steps to getting on purpose. Make the necessary changes to get in position for your purpose.

DECLARATION:

Today I get in the position of prayer and Your presence to take hold of my purpose. Thank You, God, for the Fresh Beginnings of a changed mind.

FRESH BEGINNINGS DAILY WORKSHEET

Really open your heart and allow yourself and God to take a fresh look inside. Allow the light and illumination of the Holy Spirit to shine the light of wholeness and healing into those dark places. It does not matter how long you've been on the journey--there is still a remnant of some hurt or some wound lurking around in the shadows. The following statements will help you ponder today's reading and position you to release any resentment into the hands of Jesus for Him to dispose of as He wishes. Allow yourself enough time to express it all.

I'm angry because:

I regret:

I feel sad when:

I forgive:

Now take time to reflect on today's Scripture. Write out what Jesus is speaking into your spirit:

Today I am grateful for:

My declaration for today:

#25 Through the Eyes of Christ

"To open their eyes and to turn them from darkness to light...."
(Acts 26:18)

FRESH BEGINNINGS IS really a process to help you change your mind. This exercise is to give you the support needed in knowing that a changed mind opens up great opportunities for a changed world. We've often heard "be the change you want to see." When we look at change from that perspective, our world becomes more manageable. You can clearly see that in order for the outside to change, you must deliberately, intentionally, and determinedly change the inside. When we change within, we are no longer overwhelmed with trying to change this external world.

The bigness, the chaos, and the disturbing distractions of this world can weigh heavily on us. Yet when I finally decide that I will be more loving, kinder, gentler, more giving, more understanding, stand in my own truth, and declare my own peace, my world gets lighter. Changing within allows you to make a huge deposit into the bank of humanity.

When you can look at yourself, those around you, and even the world through the eyes of Christ, you are totally transformed. You also become filled with compassion. Your level of discernment is greatly increased and your levels of judgment and criticism are greatly decreased. Begin with asking Christ what He sees when He looks at you. If nothing immediately bubbles up for you, sit with that question for a few minutes. As you sit in the silence, feel God's compassion and unconditional love for you. Allow the sensation of being enveloped in a feeling of pure acceptance. As that acceptance permeates your being, now ask that you begin to see others in that same light.

DECLARATION:

Father, I receive the gift of pure acceptance. Thank You for seeing me with eyes that promote my well-being. Thank You for the light that dispels the darkness. I am reminded that Fresh Beginnings open my eyes to the light of God.

FRESH BEGINNINGS DAILY WORKSHEET

Really open your heart and allow yourself and God to take a fresh look inside. Allow the light and illumination of the Holy Spirit to shine the light of wholeness and healing into those dark places. It does not matter how long you've been on the journey--there is still a remnant of some hurt or some wound lurking around in the shadows. The following statements will help you ponder today's reading and position you to release any resentment into the hands of Jesus for Him to dispose of as He wishes. Allow yourself enough time to express it all.

I'm angry because:

I regret:

I feel sad when:

I forgive:

Now take time to reflect on today's Scripture. Write out what Jesus is speaking into your spirit:

Today I am grateful for:

My declaration for today:

#26 Grown-up Thoughts

"When I was a child I spoke, understood and thought as a child, but when I became an adult I put the ways of childhood behind me." (1 Corinthians 13:11)

IMMATURITY CRIPPLES. THERE is nothing more frustrating than being of adult age and still making childish decisions. It's sad when we cannot choose an outfit without calling a friend for approval. Many of us still call on Mother and Father for decisions that we should be equipped to make on our own. Our views are still narrow, like children who can be selfish and often heard screaming, "It's mine and I want it now!"

Our reasoning is confused and infantile. It's even sadder when we need permission from others to be ourselves. Immaturity makes us doubt ourselves. Immaturity makes us repeat the same mistakes over and over. Immaturity makes us question our motives and keeps us standing outside of our own truth. Immaturity holds us hostage to fear and blinded to the strength that comes from stepping out of our comfort zone to take the risks that grow us up into mature adults. Immaturity keeps us disrespectful and causes us to take others for granted.

Thank God for Fresh Beginnings. It is liberating to know that at 30, 50, or 75 we can put away childish things. Thanks be to God that at any age we can learn to reason as adults. In our selected Scripture for today Paul stated that we see things in part (like children) but there will come a time when we will see clearly. To see clearly, we must make the choice to face ourselves and our God, knowing that we can safely embrace the knowledge that comes with maturity.

DECLARATION:

Thank You, Lord, for the opportunity to put away childish things and to grow up in You. The privilege of Fresh Beginnings increases my capacity to think, act, and reason as an adult.

FRESH BEGINNINGS DAILY WORKSHEET

Really open your heart and allow yourself and God to take a fresh look inside. Allow the light and illumination of the Holy Spirit to shine the light of wholeness and healing into those dark places. It does not matter how long you've been on the journey--there is still a remnant of some hurt or some wound lurking around in the shadows. The following statements will help you ponder today's reading and position you to release any resentment into the hands of Jesus for Him to dispose of as He wishes. Allow yourself enough time to express it all.

I'm angry because:

I regret:

I feel sad when:

I forgive:

Now take time to reflect on today's Scripture. Write out what Jesus is speaking into your spirit:

Today I am grateful for:

My declaration for today:

#27 Ready, Set...Wait!

"But if we hope for what we do not yet have, we wait for it patiently."
(Romans 8:25)

GETTING READY FOR an assignment or an event takes time and thought. When packing for a trip it usually involves making travel arrangements, checking the weather forecasts, and deciding what clothes and how many pairs of shoes you really need. Getting ready may also include securing adequate phone coverage, having enough money--and in some cases, emergency plans. Once we've done the preparation, we get ready for the mental or emotional stage.

Mentally and emotionally, we need to get set, or focus on the specifics of the assignment. Depending on the assignment or event, our emotions can range from very happy to very sad, from high-energy to just barely enough strength to make the journey.

Getting set emotionally is the most important aspect of this process: staying focused requires much prayer, maintaining a presence of peace, and getting rid of any negativity and anxieties. Once we're ready and once we're set, the next logical step is to go, right? Not necessarily. Getting ready and getting set are dynamics in the process. We can see the destination, we can see the purpose just down the road, the excitement and the energy have increased our momentum...and often when we feel *I can do this,* God says, "Wait." God may say, "Not yet". Why is that? God can see the end from the beginning and He may see a ditch, a pitfall, a stumbling block that you are not quite ready to manage just yet. Waiting on God places us in the position to renew and or build strength for the blessing of God's favor. We want to go in our own strength--after all, we've been called, anointed, and chosen...and God says, "I see the preparation, yet there is still another work that must be done."

DECLARATION:

Father, I'm ready and I'm set to go out into all the world and complete my assignment. Yet I wait for Your signal to proceed to the next level...the next level of Fresh Beginnings.

FRESH BEGINNINGS DAILY WORKSHEET

Really open your heart and allow yourself and God to take a fresh look inside. Allow the light and illumination of the Holy Spirit to shine the light of wholeness and healing into those dark places. It does not matter how long you've been on the journey--there is still a remnant of some hurt or some wound lurking around in the shadows. The following statements will help you ponder today's reading and position you to release any resentment into the hands of Jesus for Him to dispose of as He wishes. Allow yourself enough time to express it all.

I'm angry because:

I regret:

I feel sad when:

I forgive:

Now take time to reflect on today's Scripture. Write out what Jesus is speaking into your spirit:

Today I am grateful for:

My declaration for today:

#28 The Wait List

"Wait on the Lord and be of good courage, and He shall strengthen your heart…." (Psalm 27:14)

FOR MOST OF us, waiting is a frustrating experience. We've gotten to the point where we don't want to wait for anything. We want fast food, fast relationships, fast money, fast cars, overnight mail…seems we are in a hurry for everything! Of course, we've been overwhelmed with messages that we need to get things done now. Make your decisions now. Make your choices now. It doesn't matter if the decision is the best one or the right one--just make a decision and clean up the mess later.

But I've come to realize that there are many good things that come from waiting. The author of the above text states that waiting on the Lord brings good courage. In today's world, where we are bombarded with so much negativity, we need good courage to face the day that awaits us. He also reminds us that waiting will give us strength. Waiting supplies the necessary strength that sustains us and supports us under the heavy load of life. When life is pushing you to get it done and get it done right here and right now, remind yourself to wait. Remember that waiting brings clarity when faced with a difficult decision. Remember that waiting also brings comfort and peace when we've lost our way. Let us put our names on the wait list as we wait for God to either move on our behalf or show us our next steps. Lately it has become a fun adventure to wait for items to come in the snail mail. Waiting increases the anticipation of when it will arrive and then opening the package with excitement. Waiting has become a fulfilling event in itself. As I wait on the Lord, my courage and strength are increased to levels that line up my heart's desires with God's desires for me.

DECLARATION:

Father, I place my name on Your wait list. I am content to wait on Your move in my life. I calmly wait for a fresh word to usher in the experience of Fresh Beginnings.

FRESH BEGINNINGS DAILY WORKSHEET

Really open your heart and allow yourself and God to take a fresh look inside. Allow the light and illumination of the Holy Spirit to shine the light of wholeness and healing into those dark places. It does not matter how long you've been on the journey--there is still a remnant of some hurt or some wound lurking around in the shadows. The following statements will help you ponder today's reading and position you to release any resentment into the hands of Jesus for Him to dispose of as He wishes. Allow yourself enough time to express it all.

I'm angry because:

I regret:

I feel sad when:

I forgive:

Now take time to reflect on today's Scripture. Write out what Jesus is speaking into your spirit:

Today I am grateful for:

My declaration for today:

#29 Living the Lie of Someone Else's Journey

"Master, who did sin, this man or his parents, that he was born blind?" (John 9:2)

UNTIL I ESTABLISH my own identity in Christ, I will continue to live the life someone else has declared for me. As children, we have no choice but to believe what our parents or other caregivers tell us about our life, our situations, and our truth. Also as children we have no choice but to embrace that truth as our own. Sadly, someone else's truth hardly ever fits the truth God has destined for us. Even sadder is that our identity is so wrapped up in the connection with our parents/caregivers that we consider it dishonorable to disagree with the words they spoke. What's worse is that if we discard those faulty declarations, we feel isolated and different from the family. So we hold on to the lie. We covenant with the lies that steal, kill, and even destroy.

The disciples were trying to come up with a reason for why a man was born blind. Was it something his parents did, and now he must suffer the consequences? Thank God for Jesus! He replaced the lie with truth and gave this man his eyesight to the glory of God. Even this man may have felt that his blindness was the result of his parents' folly. This man could now "see" for himself and begin to declare his own truth in Jesus. Get off the fast track of someone else's journey. Stop believing the lie of someone else's journey. Get on your journey with the Lord and watch Him peel back the layers of lies and reveal the great truth at the core of who you are. You are a beloved child of God, Who knows all your comings and goings. Praise the God who fearfully and wonderfully made you! The truth is that I am the one Jesus died for, and that He has made a way for me to live the truth of my own journey.

DECLARATION:

Dear God, what a blessing to be free from the lie someone else has spoken over my life. Today's Fresh Beginnings start with my declaration of my truth.

FRESH BEGINNINGS DAILY WORKSHEET

Really open your heart and allow yourself and God to take a fresh look inside. Allow the light and illumination of the Holy Spirit to shine the light of wholeness and healing into those dark places. It does not matter how long you've been on the journey--there is still a remnant of some hurt or some wound lurking around in the shadows. The following statements will help you ponder today's reading and position you to release any resentment into the hands of Jesus for Him to dispose of as He wishes. Allow yourself enough time to express it all.

I'm angry because:

I regret:

I feel sad when:

I forgive:

Now take time to reflect on today's Scripture. Write out what Jesus is speaking into your spirit:

Today I am grateful for:

My declaration for today:

#30 I Am

"Let the weak say I am strong." (Joel 3:10)

WHATEVER FOLLOWS YOUR statement "I am…" is coming after you. The author of that statement made a powerful and profound statement of truth. I've heard it in several places and recognize the powerful impact of saying "I am" has on what will eventually manifest in my life. The first time I heard the power of "I am" was just about thirty years ago when the preacher proclaimed, "God says my name is 'I am,' and 'I am' means He is whatever you need Him to be!" Since that time it occurred to me to be very careful of the words that were coming out of my mouth. One of the most powerful lessons of the "I am" is knowing that if I just change my mind I can change the words I choose to speak into my life. This thought led to the revelation that my thoughts and words are powerful enough to change my situations. Change your mind from the deeply buried patterns of thinking and speaking negatively to proclaiming I am healed, I am prosperous, I am loving, and I am loveable…and witness the immediate effect on your mood, your belief system, and eventually your behaviors.

Another powerful lesson is learning to intentionally guard your thoughts, words, and feelings. For every time you speak in the negative concerning your life affairs, you speak defeat, lack, and frustration into your life. Speaking in the negative is limiting. However, knowing that you can express the power of "I am" to unleash great and amazing potential to change your world is liberating. It makes sense that regardless of what has been poured into your spirit by yourself and others, you would begin to see the value of speaking life-giving words into your life. When you speak or think "I am," you release the movement and action of God to express into your life. Declaring "I am" releases the presence and power of God to show up as blessings, favor, security, peace, and all the good you would have to come into your life.

DECLARATION:

Father, I am declaring the Fresh Beginnings of a new mind, new words, and new behaviors. I am walking in the newness of life, starting today.

FRESH BEGINNINGS DAILY WORKSHEET

Really open your heart and allow yourself and God to take a fresh look inside. Allow the light and illumination of the Holy Spirit to shine the light of wholeness and healing into those dark places. It does not matter how long you've been on the journey--there is still a remnant of some hurt or some wound lurking around in the shadows. The following statements will help you ponder today's reading and position you to release any resentment into the hands of Jesus for Him to dispose of as He wishes. Allow yourself enough time to express it all.

I'm angry because:

I regret:

I feel sad when:

I forgive:

Now return and reflect on today's Scripture. Write out what Jesus is speaking into your spirit:

Today I am grateful for:

My declaration for today:

#31 Grateful

"Let the peace of God rule in your heart...and be thankful." (Colossians 3:15)

JOURNALING IS A great and popular way to keep track of all the things you are grateful for on a daily basis. Remembering all the acts of kindness you receive as well as those you shower onto others is a powerful indicator of the connection we have to each other. Gratitude is also a way of showing up that speaks volumes about your decision to live peacefully with yourself and humanity.

One of the more beautiful aspects of gratitude is that the great majority of the things we are grateful for are free. A smile, holding hands, holding the door for someone, looking out for a neighbor, and praying for someone are poignant expressions of the spiritual maturity needed to recognize the all-encompassing love available to everyone. When you stand in the place of gratitude, you are first reminded of the goodness of God toward you. Next you are grateful that your gifts can serve another. Nothing heals the wounded spirit like an act of kindness extended to someone in pain, whether it is physical or emotional. Another important aspect of being grateful is that you don't have to earn or work for it. Many things happen because we have created a space for that act to show up. How? By remembering to be grateful for everything that comes your way. Being grateful through difficult challenges are dynamic lessons that increase your strength and wisdom to handle future challenges. I am grateful for gifts that bless others linking our spirits in the never-ending chain of gratitude.

DECLARATION:

God, I am immensely and eternally grateful for the gift of Fresh Beginnings.

FRESH BEGINNINGS DAILY WORKSHEET

Really open your heart and allow yourself and God to take a fresh look inside. Allow the light and illumination of the Holy Spirit to shine the light of wholeness and healing into those dark places. It does not matter how long you've been on the journey--there is still a remnant of some hurt or some wound lurking around in the shadows. The following statements will help you ponder today's reading and position you to release any resentment into the hands of Jesus for Him to dispose of as He wishes. Allow yourself enough time to express it all.

I'm angry because:

I regret:

I feel sad when:

I forgive:

Now return and reflect on today's Scripture. Write out what Jesus is speaking into your spirit:

Today I am grateful for:

My declaration for today:

Meet the Author

Dr. Gwendolyn L. Pettway is the founding pastor of The Full Gospel Christian Church (Disciples of Christ) of Detroit, Michigan which began ministry in 2005. Full Gospel is the manifestation of many years as interim and permanent pastor for several Disciple Churches in the Metro Detroit area.

She is currently a senior staff therapist with the Grace Counseling Center of Detroit where she specializes in marital conflict resolution, depression, anxiety, low self-esteem, and family and individual counseling.

Dr. Pettway is often requested as a lecturer and workshop facilitator, presenting such topics as *Depression, The Gift of Relationship, Self-Esteem (Temple or Trash Can?), Divorce Recovery, Managing Grief, Mother-Daughter DIS-Connect* and many other areas of life experience. Dr. Pettway is also trained as an Imago Relationship Therapist.

Dr. Pettway is an associate professor with Heritage Center for Religious Studies where she teaches *Christian Counseling, Pastoral Care,* and *Preaching Eulogies*.

Ministry to the wounded and hurting is her passion, as she seeks to help God's people understand who they are in Him. Contact information:

Full Gospel Christian Church (DOC)
18101 James Couzens Fwy.
Detroit, MI 48235
Revgwen50@sbcglobal.net

CPSIA information can be obtained
at www.ICGtesting.com
Printed in the USA
FFOW02n0411270916
27993FF